P9-DIW-631

LEVEL 2

# Sea Turtles

Laura Marsh

NATIONAL GEOGRAPHIC

Washington, D.C.

**For Eliza**
**—L. F. M.**

Copyright © 2011 National Geographic Society
Published by National Geographic Partners, LLC, Washington, D.C. 20036. All rights reserved.
Reproduction in whole or in part without written permission of the publisher is prohibited.

Design by Yay Design

Paperback ISBN: 978-1-4263-0853-6
Hardcover ISBN: 978-1-4263-0854-3

cover, Masa Ushioda/www.coolwaterphoto.com; 1, Carson Ganci/Design Pics/Corbis; 2, Frans Lanting/NationalGeographicStock.com; 4-5, Aquascopic/Alamy; 6-7, Jason Isley, Scubazoo/Getty Images; 8, Jason Isley, Scubazoo/Getty Images; 10, Image Quest Marine; 11 (top), Doug Perrine/SeaPics.com; 11 (bottom), Luiz Claudio Marigo/naturepl.com; 12 (top), James D. Watt/SeaPics.com; 12 (bottom), George Burba/Shutterstock; 13 (top), Doug Perrine/SeaPics.com; 13 (bottom), Image Quest Marine; 14, Doug Perrine/naturepl.com; 15, Mitsuaki Iwago/Minden Pictures; 16, Wild Wonders of Europe/Zankl/naturepl.com; 18, Jason Bradley; 20, Doug Perrine/naturepl.com; 21, Frans Lemmens/Getty Images; 22, Luciano Candisani/Minden Pictures; 23 (top), Nils Bornemann/iStockphoto.com; 23 (bottom), Norbert Wu/Getty Images; 24, Jeffrey L. Rotman/Corbis; 25, Jim Richardson/NationalGeographicStock.com; 26, Julie Dermansky/Corbis; 27, 28, 29 (top), Audubon Nature Institute, New Orleans; 29 (bottom), Heather Stanley, Audubon Nature Institute, New Orleans; 30 (top), Frank and Helena/Getty Images; 30 (bottom), Gorilla/Shutterstock; 31 (top), hardcoreboy/iStockphoto.com; 31 (center), Stacie Stauff Smith Photography/Shutterstock; 31 (bottom), Tim Platt/Getty Images; 32 (top left), Vlue/Shutterstock; 32 (top right), Doug Perrine/SeaPics.com; 32 (left center), Wild Wonders of Europe/Zankl/naturepl.com; 32 (right center), Mitsuaki Iwago/Minden Pictures; 32 (bottom left), Stephen Frink/Getty Images; 32 (bottom right), Jason Isley, Scubazoo/Getty Images

**National Geographic supports K–12 educators with ELA Common Core Resources.**
**Visit natgeoed.org/commoncore for more information.**

Printed in the United States of America
17/WOR/9

# Table of Contents

A Sea Turtle! . . . . . 4
Ocean World . . . . . 6
Meet the Turtles! . . . . . 10
Nestbuilding . . . . . 14
Oh, Baby! . . . . . 16
Big and Small . . . . . 20
On the Menu . . . . . 22
Danger! . . . . . 24
Sea Turtle Rescue . . . . . 26
Safekeeping . . . . . 30
Glossary . . . . . 32

# A Sea Turtle!

Green sea turtle

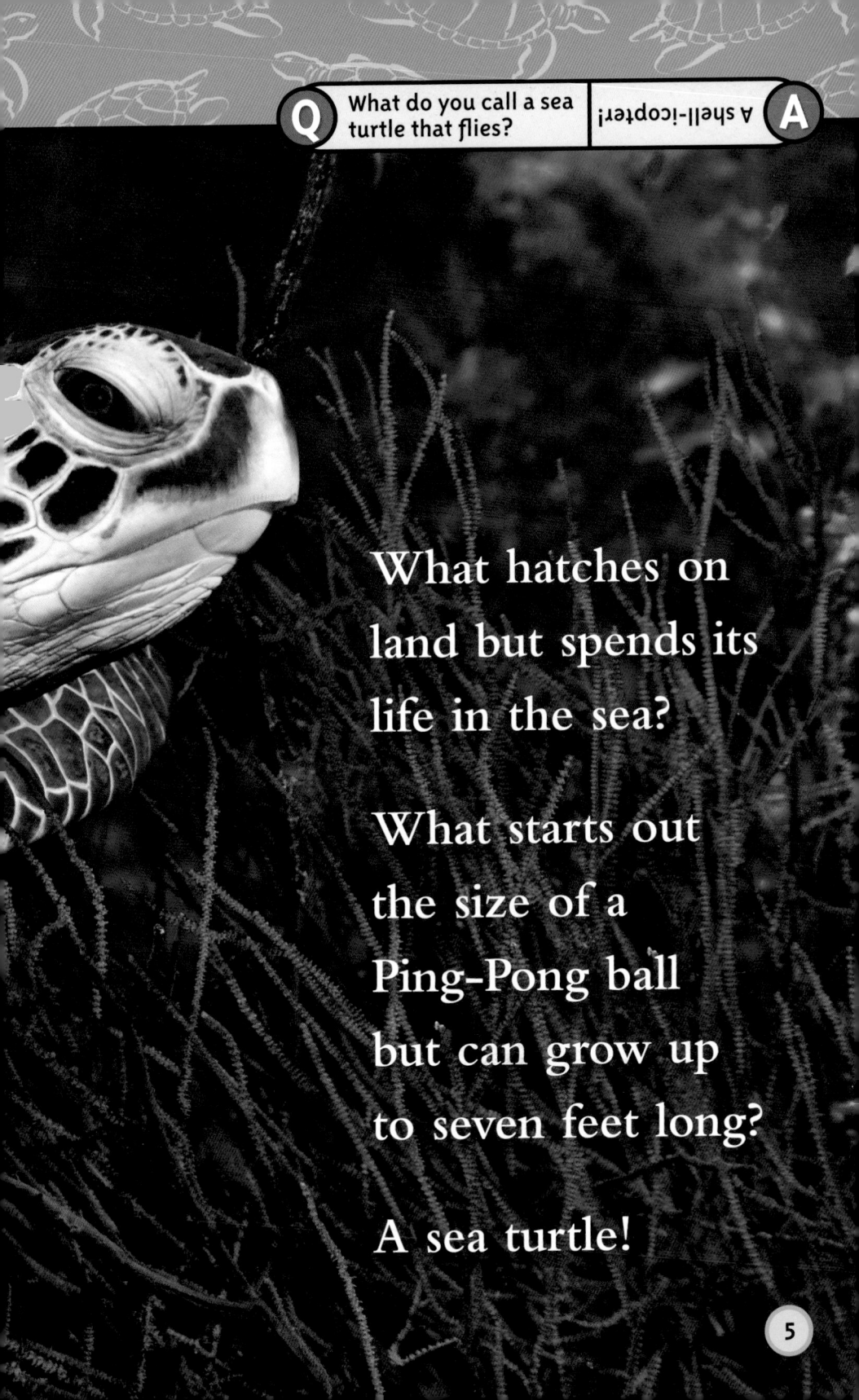

**Q** What do you call a sea turtle that flies?

**A** A shell-icopter!

What hatches on land but spends its life in the sea?

What starts out the size of a Ping-Pong ball but can grow up to seven feet long?

A sea turtle!

Sea turtles are graceful swimmers in the water. Their flippers move like wings.

**Turtle Term**

**REPTILE: A cold-blooded animal that lays eggs and has a backbone and scaly skin**

**The dark blue area shows where sea turtles travel.**

A sleek body helps the turtle move easily through the water.
The scales on its shell are called scutes.
The back flippers steer the turtle as it swims. They are also used to dig nests in the sand.
Green sea turtle

Q What kind of jokes do sea turtles tell?
A Shell-arious ones!
A sea turtle has lungs because it breathes air. A sea turtle holds its breath underwater.
Sea turtles can't pull their heads and limbs into their shells like land turtles can.
Their large, powerful flippers act like paddles.
Scientists believe some sea turtles live 80 years or more, but they don't know for sure.

# Meet the Turtles!

The loggerhead is the most common sea turtle in the southeastern United States. It gets its name from its large head.

There are seven kinds of sea turtles in the world. Each has special features.

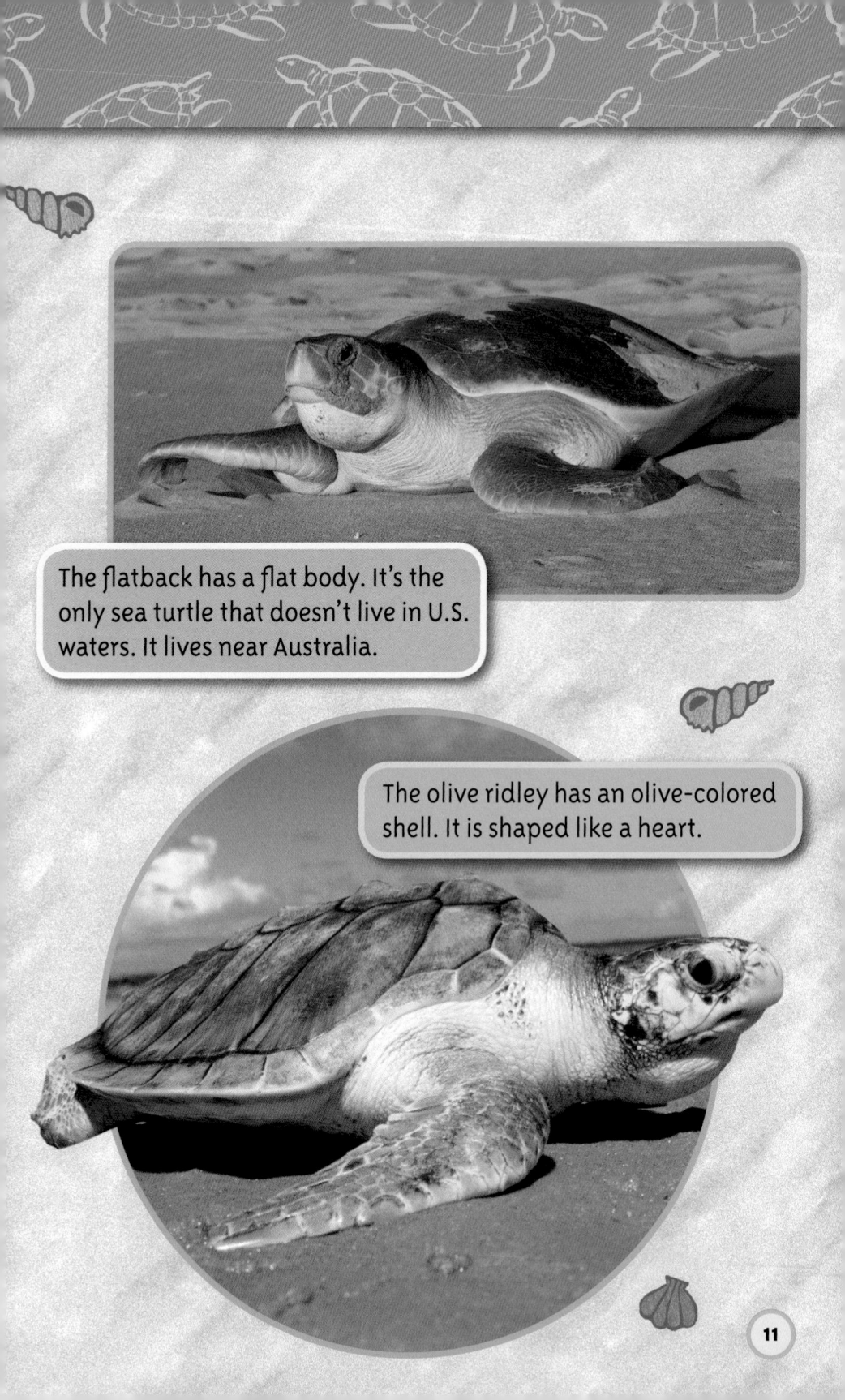

The flatback has a flat body. It's the only sea turtle that doesn't live in U.S. waters. It lives near Australia.

The olive ridley has an olive-colored shell. It is shaped like a heart.

The hawksbill can't dive deep. It spends most of its time on the water's surface.

The green turtle has a small head. Unlike other sea turtles, it goes ashore to warm itself in the sun.

The Kemp's ridley likes shallow waters. It's the world's most endangered sea turtle.
Turtle Term
ENDANGERED: At risk of dying out
The leatherback doesn't have a hard shell. Its skin is rubbery with small bones underneath.

# Nestbuilding

Female olive ridley sea turtles

A female sea turtle comes on land to lay her eggs. She usually returns to the same beach where she hatched.

Scientists aren't sure how sea turtles know where to go. They think sea turtles know by instinct.

Q What did the egg say to the other egg?

A Let's get cracking!

The sea turtle digs a hole with her back flippers. She lays her eggs and covers them with sand. Then she returns to the sea.

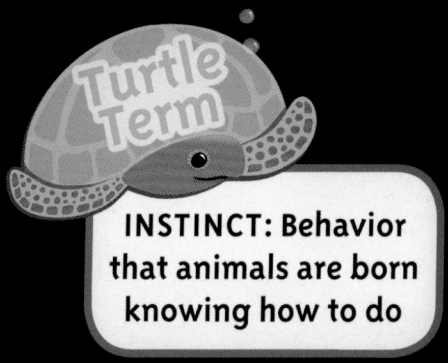


Female green sea turtle

# Oh, Baby!

**CRAAACK!** The eggs hatch after 50 to 70 days. Tiny turtles called hatchlings crawl out of their eggshells.

Turtle Term

**HATCHLING:** A young animal that has just come out of its egg

Baby loggerhead sea turtle hatching from its shell

Hatchlings usually crawl toward the sea at night. In the dark, they are hidden from predators.

The little turtles follow the brightest light. The line where the sky meets the sea is the brightest natural light on a beach.

If the hatchlings follow this light, they will make it to the sea.

**Q** What do you get when you cross a turtle and a porcupine?

**A** A slowpoke!

Leatherback hatchling

# Big and Small

The smallest sea turtles are the Kemp's ridley and the olive ridley. Adults are about two feet long and weigh up to 100 pounds.

Kemp's ridley sea turtle

Leatherback sea turtle

The largest sea turtle is the Leatherback. It can grow up to seven feet long and weigh more than 2,000 pounds. That's about ten men put together!

# On the Menu

Green sea turtle

Munch, munch, what's for lunch?

Most sea turtles eat plants and animals. They dine on algae (AL-gee) and sea grasses. They also munch on crab and conchs.

**Turtle Term**

**ALGAE: Simple, non-flowering plants that do not have stems, roots, or leaves**

Jellyfish are a favorite food for many sea turtles. But plastic trash can look like jellyfish in the ocean, and that spells trouble! Swallowing trash can hurt and even kill sea turtles.

Green sea turtle

Hawksbill sea turtle caught in a net

Trash isn't the only danger to sea turtles. Fishing nets and hungry animals can harm them, too.

**Q** What kind of phone does a sea turtle have?

**A** A shell phone!

Building lights confuse hatchlings so they don't reach the sea.

Leatherback sea turtle confused by city lights

Sometimes people even step on sea turtle nests by accident.

# Sea Turtle Rescue

In 2010 a giant oil spill leaked into the Gulf of Mexico. Oil covered sea animals and washed up on beaches. Oil is dangerous to people and wildlife.

Oil on beaches in Louisiana

Oil-covered Kemp's ridley

People in charge of a sea turtle rescue program in Louisiana saved many sea turtles.

The rescuers cleaned the turtles and gave them medicine. People cared for them until they could return to the sea.

Kemp's ridley sea turtle

# Safekeeping

You don't need to work at a sea turtle hospital to help sea turtles. Here are a few things you can do to keep them safe.

Pick up trash on the beach.

Don't release balloons into the air. (They often end up in the sea.)

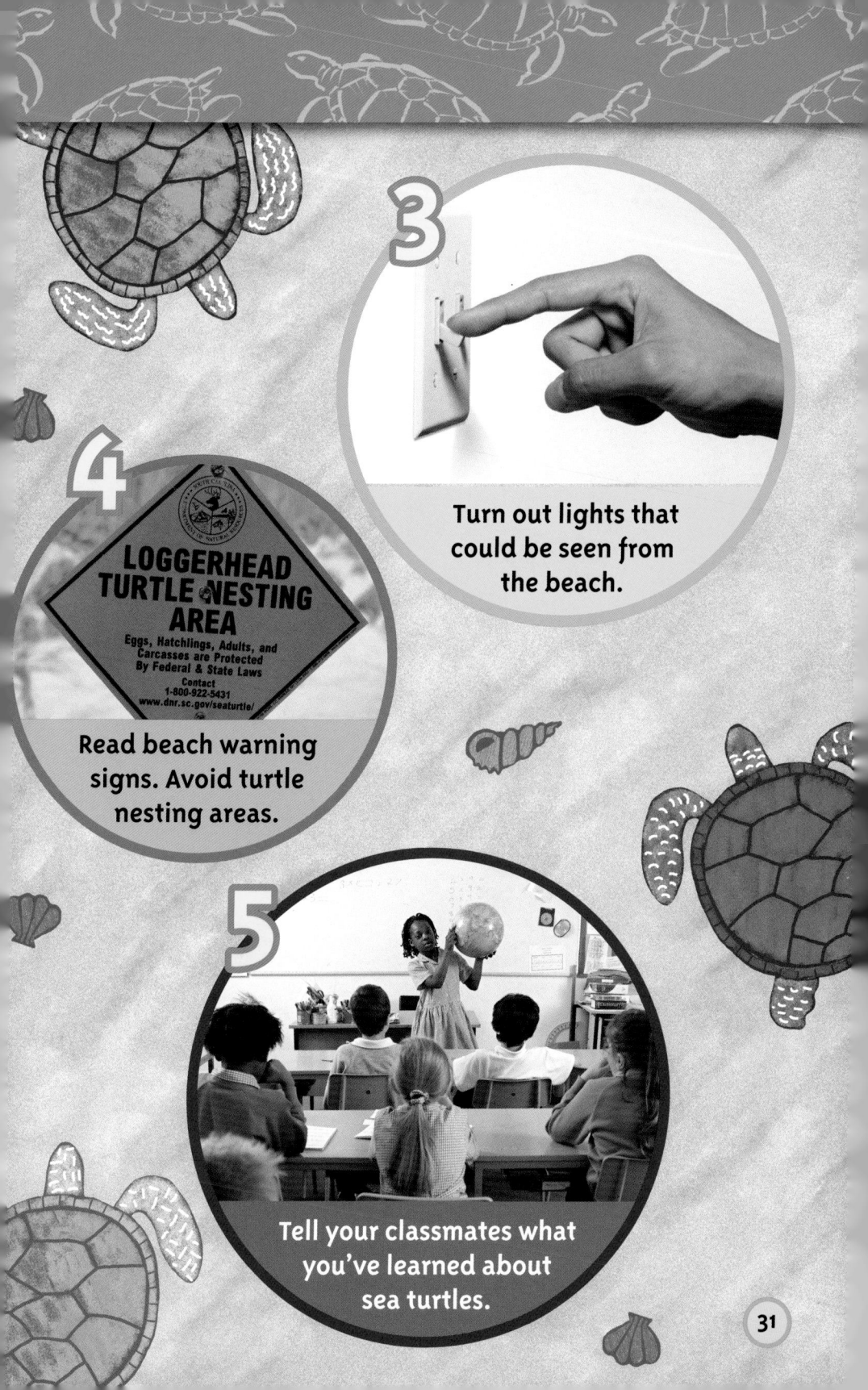
3
Turn out lights that could be seen from the beach.
4
LOGGERHEAD TURTLE NESTING AREA
Eggs, Hatchlings, Adults, and Carcasses are Protected By Federal & State Laws
Contact
1-800-922-5431
www.dnr.sc.gov/seaturtle/
Read beach warning signs. Avoid turtle nesting areas.
5
Tell your classmates what you've learned about sea turtles.

# Glossary

**ALGAE:** Simple, non-flowering plants that do not have stems, roots, or leaves

**ENDANGERED:** At risk of dying out

**HATCHLING:** A young animal that has just come out of its egg

**INSTINCT:** Behavior that animals are born knowing how to do

**PREDATOR:** An animal that eats other animals

**REPTILE:** A cold-blooded animal that lays eggs and has a backbone and scaly skin